The Algorithmic Investor

or

How I Learned to [Mostly] Stop Worrying and Get Rich [Mostly] Doing Nothing

~

By Michael Epp

Architect

AIBC

~

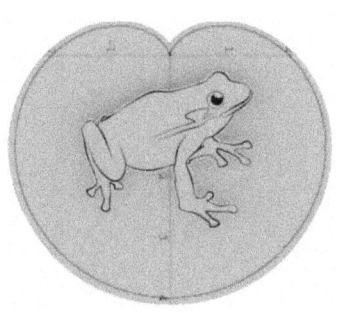

This book is lovingly dedicated

To the Memory of

William Randle Iredale

A Man among Men

And a damned fine Architect too

1. Preface

Lo and behold! Just what the world needs! Another book on investing!

Those of you who have read investing books in the past will immediately recognize that *The Algorithmic Investor* is in its title tipping its hat to one of the great classics of investing theory: *The Intelligent Investor*, by Benjamin Graham[1]. Benjamin Graham was the teacher of Warren Buffett. And if you don't know who Warren Buffett is, this must be the first book you've ever read on investing.

I'm flattered. A good time and place to start!

I have 2 main reasons for writing this book; although, like many works of non-fiction [and fiction], it could easily be distilled into several pages, or perhaps a lengthy newspaper article[2].

First, because it appears in book form, you are more likely to take it seriously. If it were printed on newsprint, you'd be far less likely to do that. You could easily wrap a fish in it, or use it to line a bird cage or start a fire. You shouldn't.

---

[1] I had another idea for a title, 'The Little Book of Algorithmic Investing', which was a nod to *The Little Book of Common Sense Investing*, another classic, though essentially a rehash of Graham's book, in my view.

[2] If you don't believe me, refer to Appendix I, below. And ignore the stupid headline. It should read more like, 'He Has Profited Handsomely by Rigorously Applying a Simple Algorithm'.

Second, because I feel I have a debt to repay. As Isaac Newton put it, 'If I have seen further than others, it is by standing upon the shoulders of giants'. What I am about to describe to you is the distillation of what I have learned from thinkers far greater than I[3]. This book is yet another grain of sand on a great heap of investment theory and knowledge. And if, like a grain of sand, it somehow lodges itself in your consciousness and irritates you into taking your financial future into your own hands, it will have done its work.

This is a fairly short book for one simple reason: it contains everything I know about investing, which isn't that much.

Before you throw this book away in disgust, however, consider this: my investment returns over the last 15+ years are about 14% compounded annually. If that number doesn't impress you, it should. It compares favourably with the kind of returns you'd get – if you were lucky – from a professionally managed investment account or mutual fund. Anyone who tells you otherwise is talking through her leopardskin pillbox hat, and more than likely, trying to get her hands on your money so she can 'manage' it for you and make herself (not you) rich in the process.

---

[3] Daniel Kahneman and Nassim Taleb, to name but two. More on them below. And if I mangle their concepts in this book, my apologies, in advance. I'm just not as smart as they are.

Bear in mind that compound returns of 20% or 30% a year, sustained, are basically unicorns[4]. Anyone who promises you this kind of return on a recurring basis is essentially promising you that you'll eventually control most of the money in the world. Needless to say, no one ever does that [I owe that last observation to Patrick McKeough].

Which reminds me of a (true) story, the first of several which you'll find throughout this text. I have a good friend who earns his living as an investment adviser (an even more thankless task than that of professional architect, in my view). One year he got his client a 30% return and the guy verbally abused him, saying "I could have gotten 50% somewhere else". So my friend said, great, if someone else can get you 50%, go to him, by all means, and he held the door open for him. You guessed it: a year later the guy was back, with his tail between his legs. And so it goes.

Consider that 14% compounded means that, using Einstein's (yes, *that* Einstein) 'Rule of 72'[5], you'll be doubling your money about every 5 years. Sound good? Read on.

---

[4] See Appendix II.

[5] An easy rule to learn. Take your projected percentage return and divide it into 72. This gives you the approximate number of years until your money doubles. That's Einstein. A real gift for taking the complex and making it simple. E=mc2 also comes to mind.

2. Where To Start?

Start at the beginning, dummy!

The beginning means simply this: get your hands on some cash to invest.

In my case, I did it by not owning a car. You've heard the expression 'Penny Wise and Pound Foolish'.

Don't do that! Be Pound Wise and Penny Foolish.

This is the first of many counterintuitive concepts you will find liberally-sprinkled throughout the text.

In any case, if you've read about investing before, you've heard about 'the latte factor'[6] or some such. All well and good, but to get where you're trying to go you'll need to do quite a bit better than that, and as quickly as possible.

This is the shortest chapter in the book, and the most straightforward. If you can't, or won't, do what you are being told right here you don't really need to read the rest of the book, because it will likely remain purely of academic interest, though you will still learn a lot worth knowing.

When I suggest being Pound Wise and Penny Foolish, I'm only being half contrarian. The weight lifters say 'no pain, no gain', and I say the same. Save until it

---

[6] The basic idea being that you skip your daily latte, invest the money saved, and go from there. You're saving maybe five dollars a day, or $1500 a year. You need to do better, and you can.

hurts. No car? No problem! Take the bus, and pocket the difference. Right away you're up 10k a year. Save it, and invest it. Own a house? Rent out a room and invest the income. Have a marketable skill that you enjoy employing? Use it in your off-hours to generate some extra income and earmark it all for investment[i].

I won't belabour the point further. I'm starting to bore myself, and therefore you, too, presumably. Besides, we have bigger fish to fry, and I believe I promised that this would be a short book.

All of these suggestions **will** involve sacrifice of some kind, whether of time, convenience, putting up with an annoying roommate, or what have you. Those are the breaks.

(By the way, those are *always* the breaks. 13-year-old George Harrison played the guitar until his fingers bled; Paul Cezanne slashed his canvases to shreds in frustration; Terry Fox ran a marathon a day until his body gave up on him; George Lucas persisted with the production of the first Star Wars film in spite of the utter incomprehension of the entire cast and crew. Getting somewhere in life takes grit).

There's no way around it: some sacrifice is called for. Doing what you are doing – taking charge of your financial future – is a heroic act, which is, by definition, a lonely act. Therefore, treat yourself to a latte (at the local, *independently owned* coffee shop) when you feel like it. This is a small outlay you can easily manage, and the money you are spending is going directly into the pockets of your friends and neighbours. They have to live too, after all.

If you spend your money on a new car or flat screen TV, where is it going? Likely, into the pockets of people far away, and investors like me (insert evil laughter here)[7]. Pretty soon, your pocket too. I don't own a car, and haven't for thirty years, but I own car company and oil stocks. Starting to get the idea?

If you can save 10% of your annual net income to invest, through good years and bad, you'll start to see progress in a few short years. If you can save 20%, so much the better.

It's worth considering this: as the late great Joe Dominguez[8] said, 'You are a business'.

What do businesses do? They provide a service and aim to make a profit. If you have a job, you are providing a service. You are a business; therefore, you should aim to make a profit. If it's only 2% or 5% some years, so be it. But aim for 20.

---

[7] Unless you live next to a car factory, in which case you have my permission to buy a car, and save your investing money in some other way.

[8] The author of *Your Money or Your Life*. Another highly recommended read.

2. Wealth – A True Story

Way back when I was a young man of 40, a stripling, a neophyte, a mere poser, I read a story in the Globe and Mail Business section. I had recently started to do this, after many years of proudly reading every section *but* Business [I was an artist]. Fake news aside – because the internet was young, and newspapers still held sway – you'll have to take my word for its veracity, unless you're prepared to dig through the archives and find it.

There was a man who lived in Nova Scotia. A dyed in the wool eccentric, he rode around town on a battered old bike, slept on the floor of his house in a sleeping bag, and did odd jobs for money. He had no family to speak of, and appeared to be happy and content living alone in his little house[9].

When he died he left an estate worth $3 million. All of it was held in Bank of Nova Scotia stock. Like a good Nova Scotian, he was patriotic in his investing. It turned out that every time he had fifty bucks, he bought another share or two of stock; and never sold [his life lay elsewhere].

All the proceeds of the estate were left to The Boy Scouts and The Humane Society.

My hero.

---

[9] There's no woman in this story; a fact which may be germane. But, once again, I digress.

4. Wealth – A Fable

A frog's sitting motionless on a lily pad. A fly flies past. Almost faster than the eye can see, the frog zaps the fly and swallows it.

My question to you: was the frog 'sitting around doing nothing', or was he hunting flies?

I feel a fable coming on.

The hell with it, let's skip straight to the moral.

You'll do as well as an investor, and likely much better, if you do nothing, than you will if you actively chase investment returns.

Sounds easy, doesn't it?

Well, it isn't. If it were, everyone would do it, and we'd all be rich. (Not only that, but most investment professionals, as a class, would be out of work overnight – and nor would you need this book).

This is the crux of the book, folks (and it's only p 11!).

More on this below – after a short digression on setting up an investment account – but for now I want you to imagine yourself as that frog, who's worn himself out hopping around chasing flies, to no avail, and has decided to sit tight for awhile and see if that gets him anywhere.

It does.

5. Step Two: Spend 10 Minutes and Fill Out a Form

Okay, you've made it this far. You've gotten your mitts on let's say $5k[10]. Congratulations! You've already done better than most of your peer group, no matter what age you are.

Your next step is much easier.

You go online and download the forms for a self-directed investment account[ii]. Whether this is an RRSP, TFSA, or plain vanilla investment account is your call. You can easily open all three types of accounts at the same time; I did.

I'm mostly in RRSPs with some TFSAs. RRSPs were the flavour du jour when I started, but now the newspapers say that the young folks may never need to invest in RRSPs since TFSAs came in.

No matter. At the end of the day, it's still your money, under your control.

---

[10] One of the best books on investing I ever read was called 'Start with $1000'. It was written sometime in the 70s, and I picked it up at a garage sale about 20 years ago, for a buck. A thousand dollars was a significant portion of a year's income back then. Incidentally, I hope you're reading this book after you took it out of your local lending library – that's how I did most of my investment reading. But, if you did buy the book, let me take this opportunity to offer a hearty 'Thank You'. 100% of the proceeds from this book will go directly into my wallet. And, if you follow my advice, you'll never need to buy another investing book. So you can cross 'learn about investing' off your bucket list. That should be worth something.

6. A Nobel Prize Winner Provides Us Lucky ~~Dogs~~ Frogs with Some Free Investment Advice

Let me take this opportunity to introduce Daniel Kahneman, 2002 Nobel prize winner for economics.

I'm introducing him now because he wrote a book, a big book, an important book, an impressive book, called *Thinking: Fast and Slow*. You don't need to read it if you don't want to – although it is fascinating. Again, because this is intended to be a short book, I'll skip ahead to page 215 of Kahneman's book. On this page, and pages following, he proves that financial advisers, as a group, suffer from a cognitive illusion which he refers to as *The Illusion of Validity*.

Allow me to quote:

Some years ago, I had an unusual opportunity to examine the illusion of financial skill up close….it was a simple matter to rank the advisers by their performance in each year and to determine whether there were persistent differences in skill among them…

*To answer the question, I computed correlation coefficients between the rankings in each pair of years: year 1 with year 2, year 1 with year 3, and so on….I knew the theory and was prepared to find weak evidence of persistence of skill. Still, I was surprised to find that the average of the correlations was .01. In other words, zero….***The results resembled what you would expect from a dice-rolling contest, not a game of skill.*** [bold text mine]

Elsewhere, he notes: **It is clear that, for the large majority of individual investors, taking a shower and doing nothing would have been a better policy than implementing the ideas that came to their minds.** [bold text mine]

Kahneman accounts for this by identifying that the investment realm is not a valid environment for the development of skill for 2 reasons: it is not regular enough to be predictable; and, consequently, it is not possible to identify these regularities and learn from them through practice.

By contrast, realms such as chess, poker, and bridge *are* regular enough to allow the acquisition of expertise; as are firefighting, and emergency and delivery room scenarios, for example.

Anyone who has spent any time at all reading the financial pages will be familiar with the annual 'Stock Picking Contests', in which a number of experts are invited to pick a stock which they feel will outperform in the coming year. As a part of these contests, a purely random pick is introduced; they have a monkey throw a dart at the stock chart, or they run a wind-up toy over the stock chart and where it stops, that becomes the random pick.

The monkey and the wind-up toy always win.

Kahneman again:

Why are experts inferior to algorithms? One reason....is that experts try to be clever, and consider complex combinations of features in making their predictions. Complexity may work in the odd case, but more often than not it reduces validity. **Simple combinations of features are better.** *[bold text mine]*

Another reason for the inferiority of expert judgment is that humans are incorrigibly inconsistent in making summary judgments of complex information. When asked to evaluate the same information twice, they frequently give different answers....[obviously] [u]nreliable judgments cannot be valid predictors of anything.

So there you have it. All of the pertinent arguments are contained within Chapters 20-22 of Kahneman's book, an easy read [and re-read] of 35 or so pages.

Dawes observed that... complex statistical algorithm[s] add little or no value. One can do just as well by selecting a set of scores that have some validity for predicting the outcome and adjusting the values to make them comparable....a formula that combines these predictors with equal weights is likely to be just as accurate in predicting new cases as the multiple-regression formula that was optimal in the original sample. **More recent research went further; formulas that assign equal weights to all the predictors are often superior, because they are not affected by accidents of sampling.**

The surprising success of equal-weighting schemes has an important practical implication: **it is possible to develop useful algorithms without any prior statistical**

research. *Simple equally weighted formulas based on existing statistics or common sense are often very good predictors of significant outcomes.... **an algorithm that is constructed on the back of an envelope is often good enough to outdo expert judgment.** This logic can be applied in many domains....[including] the selection of stocks by portfolio managers.... [bold text mine]*

In a memorable example, Dawes showed that marital stability is well predicted by a formula:

Frequency of lovemaking - frequency of quarrels = x

You don't want 'x' to be a negative number!

7. Introducing [drum roll] Mike's Algorithm

So, here's my algorithm:

[assuming you own a portfolio of stocks spread out widely across industries, and ranging from small- to large- cap – see the next chapter][11].

Whenever a stock in the portfolio becomes overweighted by 50%, sell it back down to its normal weight in the portfolio and use the proceeds to buy more of whichever stock is the most beaten down at that moment.

Here's a simple example. Let's say I own 20 stocks, with a total value of about $40k. I'm looking at my holdings and I see that one of them – Teck.B -- has jumped to $3k.

That's an automatic sell – back down to $2k. I use the $1k proceeds from the sale to buy more of whichever stock is lagging. Let's say Torstar has dropped to $1k. So I buy more, rebalancing it back to its normal weighting of about $2k in the portfolio.

That's it – until the next time this happens, with the same, or other, stocks.

Rinse and repeat. Rinse and repeat. **No exceptions!**

It's harder than it sounds – you're selling some of a 'winner' and buying more of a 'loser'. But it works!

---

[11] See Appendix IV for my current holdings as of this writing.

8. The Algorithmic Advisor

Research -- who needs it?

We do. Mind you, we don't need that much; but we need it to come from a reliable source.

From the beginning, I've been using the TSI network[12] as my source of recommendations for portfolio construction.

My original reason for subscribing to the newsletters they offer was simple: they appeared in The Globe and Mail business section as an outstanding source of investing recommendations. That is, they made money over the long term!

At the time [2001], there was no real indication, as I recall, as to what made TSI's recommendations so good.

When I first subscribed, TSI's newsletters provided all kinds of investor information and insight. After a time, they stopped. Nobody really cared why the advice worked – they just knew they were making money. Big long back-stories were not really of interest.

---

[12] 'TSI' stands for 'the successful investor'; when I tell people this, they tend to snicker, because it sounds hokey. However, if you've been reading closely, you'll recognize the origin of the name: The Intelligent Investor – The Successful Investor – The Algorithmic Investor. Moral: Don't let a hokey name keep you from getting rich!

[This is a pretty typical characteristic of investors, incidentally. They don't ask where the money's coming from, as long as it keeps coming. This explains why they continue to invest in big tobacco, for example, and in aerospace [ie, arms]. But I digress. Again].

However, with a very nominal amount of digging, you can easily find out how TSI arrives at its stock recommendations.

You guessed it.

They use an algorithm.

We don't need to go into the details here. Suffice it to say that, just as described in the previous chapter, they apply a simple ranking system to all the stocks on the exchange – 1 point for dominance in a particular sector, 1 point for continually raising the dividend, etc. **There's no emotion or hunch-playing in the recommendations. The stocks with the highest scores win. The algorithm rules – no exceptions.**

Obviously, a simple ranking system doesn't guarantee that an individual stock will outperform – which is why you still need to diversify. But, it does pretty much guarantee that anyone who follows their recommendations sensibly can reliably outperform the professionals, and at low [and fixed] cost.

Note another thing about this investment advice: the same stocks keep coming up as 'buys' again and again, year after year. That is, once you've built your portfolio, you won't be doing much new buying. Generally, you'll just be rebalancing the stocks you already own. This, to me, was one of the most remarkable and surprising things about investing. I thought I'd be moving in and out of stocks all the time; at least monthly. Nothing could be further from the truth[13]. In general, the only times I ended up 'out of' a stock was when another company came along and bought the whole company, usually at large premium. Sleeman, Masonite and Hudson's Bay are three that come to mind.

Sleeman is perhaps the most striking example from my personal investing history. At the time, small-cap oil producers were in the news in a big way. One of my positions had been bought out so I needed a new 'buy'. I looked at my portfolio and the logical buy was Sleeman. I thought, I must be some kind of idiot, buying beer when everyone else is buying oil. I did it anyway [which was not easy]. Less than two months later, Sleeman was bought out by Sapporo at a 70% premium.

The algorithm won.

It won again last year, when Teck.B went from a low of $3.50/share to $35. I've owned the stock from the beginning, that is, for about 16 years. Over that time, it's gone as high as $70 [after the 2008 crash].

---

[13] To use an analogy, which is possibly of limited utility: if stocks were 'employees' would you fire the best and keep the worst? Obviously not, yet this is what investors all too often do.

Because I have rebalanced regularly, I have automatically bought low and sold high. I was selling it all the way up last year – 2016 was my first 'six figure' year as a result.

It's worth noting at this point that I was chatting recently with my friend the investment advisor about Teck and described how I'd been selling all the way up. He looked sheepish, and admitted that he had owned it too, but had sold his entire position and taken profits too early[14].

That's expertise for you.

Finally, note that you won't need to manage your portfolio on a weekly, or even monthly, basis. Checking and rebalancing 4 or 6 times a year is probably adequate. You have better things to do [I hope] than manage your investments[15]. And, as Kahneman demonstrated, conclusively, **the more you fiddle, the lower your returns, on average.**

So, again, I've averaged just shy of 14% for about 16 years now. Last week, the newspaper informed me that 'successful' mutual funds are 'boring'. Their definition of success? 7.5% over 20 years; 10% over 15

---

[14] A little more on this in the next chapter, ie, the myth of buying low and selling high. Optional reading.

[15] As the man said, 'life is what happens while you're busy making plans'. The same should be true of your 'Investing life'. One day you'll look at your portfolio and realize that you've arrived. It will sneak up on you, as it did me. Let me know how you do -- it took me 15 years.

years, etc. I'm a lot more boring – boredom being defined as buying, holding, and rebalancing -- than they are -- to the tune of long-term returns which are running 50 to 100% better! – and **I'm no expert.**

This information should provide adequate 'Proof of Concept' of Kahneman's findings. What you do now is up to you, and depends heavily on your ability to do what is right, even when it feels wrong....[16]

---

[16] This reminds me of another anecdote which is also widely known. Researchers put young kids in a room with a cookie. The kids, who were all about 5 years old, were told that if they sat there for 15 minutes without eating the cookie the researcher would come back and give them another cookie as a reward. The film of the kids as they resist the temptation of the cookie they *can* have, versus the delayed gratification of *two cookies*, always elicits roars of laughter from adult audiences. However, followup research indicates that later in life, the kids who successfully waited the 15 minutes did significantly better by common metrics such as high school graduation, level of post-secondary education attained, and so on. It may well be, therefore, that your investing fate was pre-determined by the time you were 5, in which case, this book is mostly a waste of ink and paper. Because, when you think about it, algorithmic investing [or investing in general] isn't really that much different from sitting alone in the room with a cookie, waiting for the additional one to arrive.

9. A Few Final Notes

The substance of this book is now concluded. You can stop reading at the end of chapter 8, apply what you've learned, and become a successful investor. Please refer to chapter 10, however, for some final advice on how to deploy your wealth.

Note that the algorithm I described can be modified by you to suit; you might, for example, wait until one of your holdings doubles in value before you sell it down. And you can get your advice from any number of providers – just make sure you are paying for advice on a fixed-cost and not a percentage basis. Once you've set up your system, though, give it time to work. You have to be patient. You have to be that frog, sitting on that lilypad – he's enjoying the sunshine while he waits for the next fly to happen by.

Below, I have a few more investing notes I am willing to share, arranged in no particular order. These are provided in response to things I've heard, read, or otherwise thought about. I hope you find them of use.

1. 'Splain, Lucy

You may be wondering how I arrived at my algorithm. Well, actually, it's a short story. Since I had to rebalance periodically without increasing my number of holdings, I ended up buying more of what I already owned, and it made sense to buy more of whatever happened to be cheapest at any given time. The 'sell when up 50% rule' evolved over time – it just felt like a good number. Less than that and it didn't make sense economically as the trading cost was too high in percentage terms; more than that and I found myself tempted to 'let profits run', which can be highly detrimental to long-term returns. Ultimately, the point is that *you have basic rules that you **never** deviate from*. This is the formula for success!

2. **Average vs. above average.**

As you've probably heard by now, most people consider themselves 'above average' drivers. Obviously, that can't be true if 'average' is a meaningful concept.

The point of this book is to make you special, in the investing realm. Whether you are special in any other is no concern of mine; though we each of us, I believe, have a unique talent some way, somehow. Warren Buffett has a talent for making lots and lots of money. He bought his first stock at 10 years of age [eesh]. That's an amazing thought, though I take the liberty of pointing out that at that age I was already a not-bad painter. Fighter planes were my specialty. If you think about it, you were probably pretty good at something by that age too. And equally likely, the adults in your life weren't paying much attention to you, which was ideal, because it gave you lots of time to work on your passion.

If you were lucky, or blessed, or dogged enough, when you became a grown-up, you carried your passion out into the big wide world and 'monetized' [I hate that word] it somehow. That's what Buffett did, that's what I did [this is where my similarity to Buffett ends]. That's what Lennon & McCartney did. That's what Edwin Lutyens did. And so on.

Some vocations are more remunerative than others. Sad, but true. At least if you follow your bliss, you won't be lying on your death bed lamenting the fact that you wasted your life. That's surely the worst fate that can befall a person[17].

To be special as an investor, you have to do the opposite of what most everyone else is doing. You already knew that – and I told you how to do it, as described above.

You're special. You're like everybody else. You decide.

3. Risk.

Investing involves risk. We all know this.

But what are the risks of not investing?

There's a way to avoid being an unsuccessful investor. That way is to not invest at all.

There'll be times when you feel sick about the way your investments are doing. That said, you should

---

[17] See Appendix III.

take a deep breath, suck it up, and get on with your life.

What's striking to me is the fact that so many people hear about my investment results and appear completely disinterested. How can they not realize the importance of what I'm telling them[18]?

I've tried to account for this in any number of ways. The best I can come up with is that people haven't invested much, or if they have, they aren't really that interested in talking about it – maybe because they're not doing very well? And they're hoping that their lacklustre results, whether in stocks or mutual funds, will at some point turn around and validate their lack of action.

And maybe if they really paid attention to their investments, and they still didn't do well, they'd feel badly about themselves, when they could just blame their investment advisor, and keep on working, buying lottery tickets, and hoping for that eventual payoff, one way or another.

Making the investment professional responsible for one's substandard results is really a cop-out. I sincerely hope you can see and admit that.

---

[18] Incidentally, Kahneman, the Nobel laureate, has run up against this too. "Facts that….threaten people's self esteem….are simply not absorbed. This is particularly true of statistical studies of performance, which provide base-rate information that people generally ignore when it clashes with their personal impressions from experience".

It has been pointed out that normally sober people who will shop extensively for a $200 pair of shoes will willingly, and without much reflection, hand over $10k on an investment they know next to nothing about. Something to reflect on – is this you?

4. Diversification.

Enron. Remember Enron? Maybe, as I do, you can recall reading stories at the time about how lots of Enron employees lost their life savings and retirement funds because they were invested in Enron stock and nothing else.

Why? Why didn't they take partial profits and diversify?

Maybe it was about greed. Or possibly they were naïve investors [which isn't really an excuse]. One story in particular comes to mind. 'I was at my father's deathbed, and on the TV in the hospital room came the news that Enron was collapsing. At that moment, I knew that I was no longer a millionaire. My life savings were gone'.

Note the sympathy play there – the deathbed scenario. Sorry, but you should have diversified. *Especially when a stock runs away – this can be a clear signal that there's something fishy going on.*

Note that the algorithmic system described in this book means that you are <u>always</u> selling on the way up. <u>That's</u> the time to be selling! If you're selling on the way down, so is everyone else! You'll get wiped out! Stay diversified at all times!

Speaking of diversification, a couple of years ago I inherited a portion of my father's estate. After paying off my outstanding debts, I split the remainder with my wife. As a joke, I transferred the money into her account without saying anything [we've always kept our finances separate, because when we met she was my landlady, ie, she owned all the assets. My net worth is now slightly higher than hers [which has taken 25 years]. But don't tell her].

She'd been after me for awhile about the fact that when our kids were small she supposedly had to spend a bunch of her savings as my income wasn't adequate to pay all the expenses of child-rearing. Whatever. I could have argued with her over it, but when I inherited the money, I put the money into her account, with interest.

I told a few people I had done this, and they were outraged. My financial advisor friend said, 'She would never have done the same for you!' [how does he know?].

But the way I looked at it, because she is all about real estate and fixed-income investing, transferring a portion of the inheritance to my wife made great sense from a diversification standpoint.

If the sky falls and I get wiped out, we'll still have roofs over our heads and some money in the bank.

Also, conduct with me a little thought experiment. Let's say I hadn't transferred the money to her, and that her resentment over the money I 'owed' her had festered to the point where she decided to sue for divorce.

A divorce would have cost me a lot more than half the inheritance would have. It would have been financially ruinous for both of us.

Viewed in that way, the money I 'gave' her was really an insurance policy, and has had the effect of significantly improving relations in the marriage.

This is another example of the 'what if' or the 'unknown unknown'. Maybe we wouldn't have divorced; or maybe a relatively small outlay now prevented huge headaches later. We'll never know. But from my point of view, giving her the money wasn't just fair-minded, it was also prudent.

Success in life is much more a matter of avoiding large losses [eg., divorce] than it is of making big gains. Having said that, if Fortune smiles on you, make the most of it! Because studies show that people not only underestimate the impact of losses, they overestimate the amount of good fortune they can reasonably expect[19].

---

[19] As discussed in *The Black Swan* by Nicholas Taleb. Another book you owe it to yourself to read, if you haven't yet.

5. Fair and Unfair.

I read somewhere recently that the stock market is yet another scheme by the rich to defraud the poor. I don't buy that. My personal experience doesn't bear that out at all.

I'm much more inclined to think that 'the market' tends to confirm your innate tendencies, regardless of your net worth.

In my life, I've almost invariably been punished for doing the right thing -- except when it came to investing. In all the years I've spent as a professional [architect], I've routinely [though not invariably] been censured for speaking plainly, whether it be to employers or clients.

It's gotten to the point that I made up a joke about this: Q: What do you call a person who speaks truth to power? A: Unemployed[20].

I also have a habit of insisting that 'simplest is best', and while clients usually nod in agreement, they end up subverting this principle, more often than not.

Because, you see, it's *their* house, and *they* know best. They've never built a house before, and their architect has been at it for thirty years – but never mind that!

---

[20] As Kahneman notes in his chapter *The Engine of Capitalism* "Experts who acknowledge the full extent of their ignorance may expect to be replaced by more confident competitors, who are better able to gain the trust of clients". ie, "Acting on pretended knowledge is often the preferred solution [to an unbiased appreciation of uncertainty]".

This time is different, and they can see this clearly! It's perfectly human [that is, entirely, tiresomely predictable] for them to feel this way [which is the first thing that should give them pause]. Unfortunately, this leads them to make ill-considered and ill-advised decisions during construction, which increases the project cost and diminishes the result.

For the professional, the deeply frustrating part of all this is that he can picture the outcome if the process had not been fiddled with [as the client cannot]. But, of course, it is futile to bring this up with the client – because the project has already been completed their way. The horse is out of the barn, and there's no getting it back in[21].

At least I'm not an investment advisor – it must be truly hellish to deal with an entire roster of clients who all insist on selling at once in a temporary down market. In this respect, at least, we architects have it easy.

Getting back to 'Fair' for a moment – there's a saying about the stock market that goes 'Bears make money, bulls make money, but pigs get slaughtered'. This saying, though common, has always been somewhat

---

[21] Kahneman again: 'In 2002, a survey of American homeowners who had remodeled their kitchens found that, on average, they had expected the job to cost $18k; in fact, they ended up paying an average of $38.5k....customers [are unable to] imagine how much their wishes will escalate over time. *They end up paying much more than they would if they had made a realistic plan and stuck to it* [italics mine]. – from Chapter 23, *The Outside View*

opaque to me. Let me hazard a guess as to its meaning: the pig is ruled by greed and therefore chases performance [like the frog did, before he wised up]. This is the fastest way to dismal investment results, and the ultimate loss of all investment assets. Hence, he ends up 'slaughtered'. By contrast, bears and bulls both have a fixed view of the market, and they stick to it; net result, profit.

6. Noise versus Signal.

Speaking of pigs: don't pay attention to the herd. That's the quickest way to get trampled. The herd makes a lot of noise [oink! oink!]. You don't want noise. Noise is useless. You want signal. **Someone else is getting rich faster than me** – that's noise. **This stock is way undervalued** – that's signal. **The Market's down today** – noise. **The Market returns 5-6%, compounded, over long periods** – signal.

Consider that the S&P 500 varies annually between -10% and +30%, with approximately 80% reliability. This means that 20% of the time, you'll be surprised, as 'Mr. Market' will be down by more than 10% [an unpleasant surprise] or up by more than 30% [a pleasant surprise]. Also, realize that these are averages. In other words, in a given year, the average stock either doubles or halves in value! The stock market is a volatile place! You need to familiarize yourself with this concept and govern your behaviour accordingly. That is, not panic and discipline yourself to think long term. Or better yet, buy quality investments and try and forget about them.

Consider that investing has been defined, quite correctly I think, as 'gambling with the odds in your favour'. That means that over a given randomly chosen period you could quite likely be in a losing position.

A study using weighted dice showed that people still managed to lose money, even when they knew the odds were in their favour! They had been coached in advance on what to do: yet, when they felt 'the chips were down', they still overreacted and ended up in a net loss position, although, by using a simple rule [aka, algorithm] they could have vastly improved their odds of ending up with a net gain [and in a certain percentage of cases, a huge gain]. The algorithm was ignored; emotion ruled; disaster ensued.

That's another reason you need to stick with your algorithm: it blocks noise. It's like the old 'keep your eye on the ball', except that in this case, it's 'the algorithm'.

7. **Time in the Market.**

That's what the pros say: it's not about **timing the market**, it's about **time in the market**. And for once, they're worth listening to.

Statistical analysis shows that, *over any given period*, if you are out of the market on the ten biggest days, you miss half your profits. Because, you see, the market doesn't just have sudden drops, it also has sudden jumps. It's a bit like the old Snakes and Ladders game in that way. If you aren't in the game, you are all too likely to miss out on a 'ladder' event.

Incidentally, I've always been 100% invested in equities, and I've reinvested all dividends as soon as they accumulated to an amount which made more buying economical [at least $1000].

People will say that this is too much risk for an old guy like me. I say that I have to take on more risk because I started late and have to make up for lost time. In general, if you have at least a 5 year timeline it makes sense to be in equities. If you will need the money any earlier than that, holding some cash is prudent.

Hopefully, in your case, you're still fairly young[22], so you can afford to be fully vested. And, you can afford to make some dumb investing mistakes. I think it likely that you will, at some point, follow your 'gut', or the advice of your brother-in-law Bob, and suffer a significant loss, before humbly returning to your algorithm. I've certainly done that on occasion [see Appendix I].

Walt Disney said he thought failing at business was a salutary experience *as long as* you were young enough to recover from it. He spoke from experience, since his business partner stole Oswald the Rabbit from him

---

[22] Life spans being what they are these days, young, for investment purposes, might be usefully defined as 'under 65'.

while he was in his twenties and left him broke. After that, he went on to create Mickey. Who remembers Oswald now?

The point of this paragraph, though, is a simple one. It will take you a certain amount of time to get where you want to go. So, there's no time to lose. The sooner you start the sooner you'll finish. I know a couple of young guys here on the Island who plan to be 'done' by the time they're 30. Good for them. If that's their goal they should surely make it by 40. As noted above, I didn't really get started until that age. But I still attained 'Freedom 55'.

8. You're Richer Than You Think

This used to be the actual slogan of one of Canada's Big Five Banks. I thought it was pure evil, though I never took the trouble to tell them I thought so. Perhaps I would have, if I had been their customer. Anyway, the slogan eventually went away. Whether because enough people objected to it or because the bank moved on, I couldn't say.

'You're Richer Than You Act'.

Now, that's a good working definition for the wealthy people I know.

My financial adviser friend once said to me, 'You'd never guess who the rich people on this island are'[23].

---

[23] We both live on an Island. Bowen Island, B.C., to be exact.

That's because they lived frugally while they were becoming wealthy, and when they became wealthy, they saw no reason to stop.

You see, living frugally [like any virtue] is its own reward. I've lived without a car for 30 years, which automatically means several things: I walk every day; I save $10k a year; I meet with and talk to all kinds of people while I am out and about; and I am automatically exposed to all kinds of randomness that I would never experience if I were by myself in a car [for 2 hours a day].

Here's an example of a random event which occurred to me while I was riding the bus to work. Two guys, both about my age, were sitting behind me, comparing financial notes. First guy: I'm trying to figure out how Angie and I can retire and live modestly. Second guy: God, I wish I hadn't renovated my house.

Lesson learned.

9. Frugal Schmugal

Charles Dickens wrote, "Income 20 pounds, expenses 19 pounds sixpence: result, happiness; income 20 pounds, expenses 20 pounds sixpence: result, misery".

That's a good basic working definition of wealth. Income > expenses = wealth.

So, if you made more money than you spent today, you're rich today. This idea derives from my working definition of an artist, which I've kicked around for a few years now. That is, if you spent time making art today, you're an artist. If you didn't spend any time making art today, you're not an artist. You *are* whatever you do *every day*. Or, for the sake of argument, 5 days out of 7.

I was taking a seminar with a working painter, and one of the other students in the class asked him. 'Do you paint every day?' The answer was 'Yes'. What answer was the student expecting? Does a plumber fix pipes every day? Of course! That's what a plumber does!

Same idea with money. If you made more money than you spent today, you're rich today. If you can do it today, you can do it tomorrow. If you can do it tomorrow, you can do it every day.

Do it enough times in a row, you'll find that you become magically relieved of the need for a 'day job', and all the unnecessary expense that that entails.

My brother-in-law was talking about his aged mother, who was, at that time, living alone and on a tiny government pension. He said, with some incredulity, 'And she's still saving money!'

Of course she was. She'd lived in Holland during WW II, after all. She knew what hardship meant, and she knew how to stretch a dollar. She remembered imminent starvation and had had her ideas about 'abundance' and 'wealth' skewed accordingly.

Recall Aesop's fable 'The Fox and the Grapes'. This is also known as The Sour Grapes story. In brief, a fox sees a tasty-looking bunch of grapes hanging overhead and after jumping up at them, without success, until he is worn out, he walks away and says to himself 'those grapes were probably sour anyway'.

The moral of the story is commonly taken to be that the fox is a sore loser. The thing is, though, that there's a non-zero chance that the fox is correct – that the grapes are, in fact, sour. Also, according to current psychological thinking, the fox's response is actually a healthy one. It allows him to stop obsessing over the grapes and get on with other things.

This can be a useful way to go through life. Didn't get the fancy car? It was probably a lemon anyway. Or some jealous a-hole would have keyed it. Didn't get the girl? She's a hopeless neurotic and you're better off without her in your life. Didn't get the promotion? You didn't need that stress anyway. There's a non-zero chance that all of these rationalizations are true.

My sister has always obsessed over her weight. My other sister once observed [with a trace of envy], 'She's trained herself not to want sweets'. And it's true – she has convinced herself that the short-term reward of the sweet dessert isn't worth the weight gain that results from overindulgence. When confronted with a piece of chocolate cake, most of us, even if we are on a diet, have a hard time avoiding the cake. My sister, however, doesn't have that problem at all. She has trained herself out of it.

As soon as you want something you're basically screwed. Unless you decide that you don't really want it after all. Then you're good to go.

It's obvious to me why people now have computers and home internet. The reason is simple: the powers that be saw that the old-fashioned TV set was flawed. True, you could use it to bombard people with ads for stuff they didn't need until you brain-washed them into buying it; but people still needed to get up off the couch, go out of the house, and make the purchase.

Now, with home internet and a computer, you can 'shop online', which is a vast 'improvement' on the old technology. You make it even easier for people to buy junk they don't need – not only that, they pay for the computer and home internet out of their own pockets! How cool is that!

Rule of thumb: when you find a deal online, and when your index finger is hovering over the mouse, ready to click 'Buy', quickly close the window. Wait 24 hours. See if you still want to make the purchase a day later. Oftentimes, you won't.

Don't worry about missing a 'deal'. Those Clearance Sales and Today Only Specials are, by and large, just ways for vendors to get rid of junk you don't need.

As the old man said, 'If we couldn't pay cash, we didn't buy it'. The only exception was the house[24].

Act poor and get rich; act rich and stay poor.

Why wouldn't I keep on living like a student? Those were the happiest days of my life.

As The Good Book says 'The last shall be first, and the first shall be last'. Or as Buffett says, 'You don't know who's naked until the tide goes out'.

10. Liquid vs. Illiquid.

This is another short paragraph. I'm just here to tell you that equities are appealing to anyone who is as lazy as I am for the following reason: they are highly liquid.

True, you could buy and rent property. But think about the time you have to spend managing it [or the money you have to spend having someone manage it for you]. The same is true of other 'hard' assets. You could keep a gold bar in your basement against incipient Armageddon, but think of all the practical difficulties this raises. Most likely, someone who's a lot meaner than you would show up at your house on Armageddon +1, stick a gun in your face, and take the gold. If Armageddon does come, 'all bets are off', as they say. As I said to my Advisor friend during the last

---

[24] He was pretty pithy, was the old man. His pre-marital advice to me: 'She won't change'. Three words. How right he was (I assume he'd learned this the hard way).

crash, half-jokingly, 'This time is different'. His response: 'If that's true, we're all fucked'.

Moreover, you can't sell off 1/8th of your house, or easily sell half your gold bar, but you can sell 1/8th of your holdings, with the click of a mouse[25], and the money's in your bank account in a day or two. How great is that!

The main reason a house is most people's main investment vehicle is that they can't panic and sell it, because they need a roof over their heads. Otherwise, many likely would. I think it's a terrible tragedy that so many people these days are 'house poor', because this is another situation of potentially tragic non-diversification. If your house is increasing in value exponentially, great, but beware of bubbles. You really owe it to yourself to have some investments apart from your house.

Speaking of real estate, an article appeared in the news a couple of weeks back. A couple in Toronto just sold their house, which they had owned for 51 years, for $400k over asking. Adjusted for inflation, they paid $73k for the house. Their asking price was about $700k. So I plugged the numbers into an online compound interest calculator. What they paid for the house, and what they sold it for, amounted to a 5.5% return, compounded, on their investment. If they had

---

[25] Although, as per Note 9, you may wish to wait 24 hours and reconsider your 'sell' move.

only gotten asking, their return would have been 4.5%. Not terribly impressive returns, are they?

11. Greed is good.

I'm just putting this out there for discussion. As you likely know, Gordon Gekko[26] said this.

Greed may have been good when he said that, sometime in the late-eighties, but since then it's gotten way out of hand.

When financial guys started dreaming up toxic investments and betting against them – legally – so that they could get obscenely rich by selling the investments as 'sound' when they were anything but, that wasn't greed anymore. That was fraud, and people should have gone to jail for it[27].

Becoming financially independent is great, but don't sell your soul to do it. Don't commit fraud. Don't be a lizard.

Luckily for you and me, it's still possible to get rich the old-fashioned way, without resorting to criminal activity. In fact, since you and I are less likely to fall

---

[26] In the movie 'Wall Street'. I guess it's pretty much self-evident why you would name a fictional financial guy after a lizard.

[27] The fact that they didn't outrages people's basic sense of fairness [it certainly outrages mine]. If people's sense of fairness is outraged often enough, the strength of society is seriously undermined, which is something we will all have to reckon with.

into the trap of believing in our own 'expertise' – because we are amateurs, and know it – we are likely to be profiting at the expense of the so-called professionals. The same guys who fleece others.

That should help you sleep well at night.

12. Invest With Me!

I'm kidding. You don't need me. All you need of me is sitting right here in your hot little hands.

However, I have fantasized about becoming an investment professional. I even designed a logo, which looks like this:

This would be on the front of the business card. I'd call it Black Box Investing [obviously].

The back of the card would look like this:

This is what's inside the box. Presumably. Because, you see, I'm the only one who knows what happens inside the box.

If you wanted to invest with me, the terms are simple: you agree to invest for at least five years; you open a trading account of your choice and give me exclusive use of the password; you do not ask for or expect any investment updates from me; at the end of 5 years I return your money and any profits earned. I take 1% of the profits. If there is no profit [unlikely] you get your balance back. In either case, you have the option to renew for another five years.

Simple, no?

10. What Do I Do Now?

Congratulations. You're rich, you clever thing[28].

What you do now is up to you.

Far be it from me to offer any more advice; you've been a lot more loyal to me than I had any right to expect when we started this exercise together.

But let's be honest here – money was never really the object, was it? Sure, we live in a 'money society', but as the thinker John Ralston Saul (yet another guy who's way smarter than me) noted, who remembers 'The Millionaire Next Door' after he's dead? His kids maybe, for a while.

No. Society remembers Socrates, Jesus of Nazareth, the Buddha, Mohammed; it remembers poor, tortured Van Gogh, who only painted for ten years; it remembers a deaf Beethoven standing on stage to rapturous applause with tears streaming down his face. It remembers Mozart, of course. None of them were noted for their riches, at the time or since[29]. Rembrandt and Vermeer died broke. Most of the holy men and deep thinkers of our culture thought a lot about suffering as the essential condition of our lives, and 'got' that material things were at best a panacea and at worst a distraction from what really matters

---

[28] Do you detect an underlying note of snark in my plaudits?

[29] And as the writer Kurt Vonnegut once remarked, 'By the time they were my age, most of the writers I admire most were dead'.

(note that 'own' and 'owe' derive from the same root word – how telling is that?)

If all you can think about is money and getting more of it – try eavesdropping on some 'adult conversations' and see how much time and energy goes into talk about money, status and real estate -- you've missed the point entirely. Money won't buy you Life. (Meanwhile notice the kids over in the corner, laughing themselves silly until the adults tell them to quiet down).

At the end of the day, becoming wealthy is a fairly trivial achievement and, in and of itself, is of little worth or enduring interest.

As Princess Leia said to Han Solo, 'If money's what you want, money's what you'll get'. That's pretty much the end of the story.

However, it may buy you the Freedom to create something valid and enduring.

Maybe you'll write that work of philosophy, paint those pictures, write those poems (you'll still have to sweat blood though. Money won't change that). Or maybe you'll see an undeveloped talent or a need that desperately cries out for your support.

Glenn Gould's father was a furrier and was affluent enough to pay $3000 a year (an astronomical sum in the 1940s) to develop his son's talent. He used his money to give the world Glenn Gould. Now that's value for money[iii]!

Let me close by quoting, verbatim, from one of the most perfect book endings ever. It's from Italo Calvino's *Invisible Cities*, and it concludes with an imagined dialogue between the Great Khan and Marco Polo. This is my suggestion about what you might do with your 'riches', as perishable and transient as they ultimately are[iv]:

He said: "It is all useless, if the last landing place can only be the infernal city, and it is there that, in ever-narrowing circles, the current is drawing us."

And Polo said: "The inferno of the living is not something that will be; if there is one, it is what is already here, the inferno where we live every day, that we form by being together. There are two ways to escape suffering it. The first is easy for many: accept the inferno and become such a part of it that you no longer see it. The second is risky and demands constant vigilance and attention: seek to learn and recognize who and what, in the midst of the inferno, are not inferno, then make them endure, give them space."

End Notes

[i] The most extreme example of this I ever encountered was back in the early 1990s. My wife and I had just sold our condo and were looking for a place to stay temporarily while we purchased a house. We looked at a one-bedroom apartment in Vancouver's West End. There were eight young men living there. In the bedroom were two bunkbeds. At any given time, four of the young men were asleep in the bunkbeds and four were off at work – like living on a submarine. If I recall correctly, they were fairly recently arrived in Canada, and were saving their money to buy a house together. I don't know what became of them, and we didn't end up renting that apartment, but I assume they are all retired by now. They certainly earned it.

[ii] In Canada, RBC Direct Investing, TD Direct Investing, BMO InvestorLine, National Bank Direct Brokerage, Laurentian Bank Discount Brokerage and Desjardins Online Brokerage, Qtrade Investor, CIBC Investor's Edge, Scotia iTrade, and Virtual Brokers. There may be others. I'm a credit union customer, so I use Credential Direct. Pretty much all of them charge less than $10 to trade, so it is efficient to start with $1000, if your rule of thumb is to pay no more than 1% on a trade, as it should be.

[iii] That reminds me of another story: "When John was about ten, he went on a bus trip by himself to visit some relatives in Birmingham. Someone had given him a cheap harmonica and he played it the whole way, driving everybody mad no doubt. But the conductor was greatly taken with him. Come back down here tomorrow morning, he said, and I'll give you a new harmonica, a really good one. John could hardly sleep that night, he was so excited. That bus conductor never knew what he started". – Mimi Smith, John Lennon's guardian.

Moral: Show kindness to a child; change the world.

[iv] Lay not up for yourselves treasures upon earth, where moth and rust doth corrupt, and where thieves break through and steal: But lay up for yourselves treasures in heaven, where neither moth nor rust doth corrupt, and where thieves do not break through nor steal: For where your treasure is, there will your heart be also. – Matthew 6, 19-21 (KJV)

Appendix I

ME AND MY MONEY
He invests like a machine, buying and selling by rule

LARRY MACDONALD
Special to The Globe and Mail
Published Friday, Feb. 24, 2017 4:53PM EST
Last updated Thursday, Mar. 02, 2017 11:41AM EST

Michael Epp

Occupation

Architect

The portfolio

A diversified selection of nearly two dozen stocks, including shares in Dorel Industries Inc., Metro Inc., 3M Co. and Verizon Communications Inc.

The Investor

Michael Epp started his portfolio 15 years ago at the age of 40. He never owned a car, which helped a lot with generating the savings to invest. Add in great returns (including reinvested dividends), and his portfolio is now well into 'six figures'.

How He Invests

"The success of my approach relies on acting like a machine or algorithm", Mr. Epp says. "This means automatically buying low and selling high."

"As soon as one of my holdings increases in value by 50 per cent," he continues, "I sell it back down to its normal weighting of 5 per cent in the portfolio and invest the proceeds in the stock which is the most beaten down of my holdings. This is harder to do than it sounds....but it becomes easier over time."

The rebalancing strategy has worked particularly well with cyclical stocks. Take mining company Teck Resources Ltd. With the dramatic ups and downs in its shares – a drop of 65 per cent in 2015 and rise of 430 per cent in 2016 – buying low and selling high has given his portfolio a big boost (while keeping risk under control by keeping Teck Resources' portfolio weight from getting too big or too small).

Diversification across industries is also important. So is having a mix of small to large cap companies, and exposure to Canadian and U.S. markets.

As for which companies to include in his portfolio, Mr. Epp follows "The Successful Investor" newsletters authored by Patrick McKeough. He says the recommendations are unbiased, as "there is no commission-based motive underlying the advice." Another plus is cost: less than 0.2 per cent of his assets.

Best Move

His best move was "Getting out of mutual funds back in 2001 and into a self-directed account with Credential Securities."

Worst Move

It was "selling a small-cap miner at a 50-per-cent loss during the 2008-09 bear market." Later, it rebounded way above his purchase price. If he had stuck to his rebalancing rule and bought more shares on the downswing, he would have made some good money instead.

Advice

"Have a system and stick to it, through thick and thin," he recommends. "This can be very hard – you have to master your emotions. A simple 'algorithmic' approach takes the emotion out of your investing. Read Daniel Kahneman's excellent book, *Thinking Fast and Slow*."

Appendix II

The Unicorn in the Garden
by James Thurber

Once upon a sunny morning a man who sat in a breakfast nook looked up from his scrambled eggs to see a white unicorn with a golden horn quietly cropping the roses in the garden. The man went up to the bedroom where his wife was still asleep and woke her. "There's a unicorn in the garden," he said. "Eating roses." She opened one unfriendly eye and looked at him.

"The unicorn is a mythical beast," she said, and turned her back on him. The man walked slowly downstairs and out into the garden. The unicorn was still there; now he was browsing among the tulips. "Here, unicorn," said the man, and he pulled up a lily and gave it to him. The unicorn ate it gravely. With a high heart, because there was a unicorn in his garden, the man went upstairs and roused his wife again. "The unicorn," he said, "ate a lily." His wife sat up in bed and looked at him coldly. "You are a booby," she said, "and I am going to have you put in the booby-hatch."

The man, who had never liked the words "booby" and "booby-hatch," and who liked them even less on a shining morning when there was a unicorn in the garden, thought for a moment. "We'll see about that," he said. He walked over to the door. "He has a golden horn in the middle of his forehead," he told her. Then he went back to the garden to watch the unicorn; but the unicorn had gone away. The man sat down among the roses and went to sleep.

As soon as the husband had gone out of the house, the wife got up and dressed as fast as she could. She was very excited and there was a gloat in her eye. She telephoned the police and she telephoned a psychiatrist; she told them to hurry to her house and bring a strait-jacket. When the police and the psychiatrist arrived they sat down in chairs and looked at her, with great interest.

"My husband," she said, "saw a unicorn this morning." The police looked at the psychiatrist and the psychiatrist looked at the police. "He told me it ate a lily," she said. The psychiatrist looked at the police and the police looked at the psychiatrist. "He told me it had a golden horn in the middle of its forehead," she said. At a solemn signal from the psychiatrist, the police leaped from their chairs and seized the wife. They had a hard time subduing her, for she put up a terrific struggle, but they finally subdued her. Just as they got her into the strait-jacket, the husband came back into the house.

"Did you tell your wife you saw a unicorn?" asked the police. "Of course not," said the husband. "The unicorn is a mythical beast." "That's all I wanted to know," said the psychiatrist. "Take her away. I'm sorry, sir, but your wife is as crazy as a jaybird."

So they took her away, cursing and screaming, and shut her up in an institution. The husband lived happily ever after.

Moral:

Don't count your boobies until they are hatched.

Appendix III

The Moth and the Star
by James Thurber

A young and impressionable moth once set his heart on a certain star. He told his mother about this and she counseled him to set his heart on a bridge lamp instead. "Stars aren't the thing to hang around," she said; "lamps are the thing to hang around." "You get somewhere that way," said the moth's father. "You don't get anywhere chasing stars." But the moth would not heed the words of either parent. Every evening at dusk when the star came out he would start flying toward it and every morning at dawn he would crawl back home worn out with his vain endeavor. One day his father said to him, "You haven't burned a wing in months, boy, and it looks to me as if you were never going to. All your brothers have been badly burned flying around street lamps and all your sisters have been terribly singed flying around house lamps. Come on, now, get out of here and get yourself scorched! A big strapping moth like you without a mark on him!"

The moth left his father's house, but he would not fly around street lamps and he would not fly around house lamps. He went right on trying to reach the star, which was four and one-third light years, or twenty-five trillion miles, away. The moth thought it was just caught up in the top branches of an elm. He never did reach the star, but he went right on trying, night after night, and when he was a very, very old moth he began to think that he really had reached the star and he went around saying so. This gave him a deep and lasting pleasure, and he lived to a great old age. His parents and his brothers and his sisters had all been burned to death when they were quite young.

Moral:

Who flies afar from the sphere of our sorrow
*   is here today and here tomorrow.*

Appendix IV

Current holdings as of March 28, 2017

Note the diversification across industries, markets, capitalizations, and risk rankings – this is vitally important. Also note that the number of holdings was increased to 25 at the beginning of the year, due to the increase in the total worth of the portfolio. It consisted of 20 stocks for many years.

Sectors:
U	Utilities
F	Financials
R	Resources & Commodities
M	Manufacturing
C	Consumer Goods & Services

Type:
Income	Income Yielding
Conserv.	Conservative Growth
Aggr.	Aggressive Growth

Capitalization:
SC	Small Cap
LC	Large Cap

Country:
US	Traded on US Exchange
CDN	Traded on Canadian Exchange

Newsletter:
TSI	The Successful Investor
WSS	The Wall Street Stock Forecaster
SPD	The Stock Picker's Digest

Security	Symbol	Type	Sector U	F	R	M	C	Type Income	Conserv.	Aggress.	Cap. SC	LC	Country US	CDN	Newsletter TSI	WSS	SPD
3M COMPANY	MMM	Equity															
ALIMENT COUCHE-TARD CL B	ATD.B	Equity															
BCE INC NEW	BCE	Equity															
BROADRIDGE FNCL SOLNS INC	BR	Equity															
CGI GRP INC CL A	GIB.A	Equity															
CHESAPEAKE ENGY CORP	CHK	Equity															
CHEVRON CORP	CVX	Equity															
CIBC	CM	Equity															
DOREL INDS INC CL B	DII.B	Equity															
EMERA INC	EMA	Equity															
FAIR ISAAC INC	FICO	Equity															
FINNING INTL INC	FTT	Equity															
GRT WST LIFECO INC	GWO	Equity															
HOME CAP GRP INC	HCG	Equity															
IMPERIAL OIL LTD	IMO	Equity															
METRO INC	MRU	Equity															
NEWELL BRANDS INC	NWL	Equity															
NISSAN MOTOR CO LTD S/ADR	NSANY	Equity															
SYMANTEC CORP	SYMC	Equity															
TECK RES LTD CL B	TECK.B	Equity															
TORONTO DOMINION BK	TD	Equity															
TORSTAR CORP CL B	TS.B	Equity															
TRANSCANADA CORP	TRP	Equity															
VERIZON COMMS	VZ	Equity															
WAL-MART STORES INC	WMT	Equity															
		25	4	5	4	6	6	7	8	10	5	20	10	15	13	6	6

Appendix V

Performance graphs. The kind that would warm the cockles of any investor's heart.

Note the big drop in 2008. What to do? Ignore it and get on with your life.

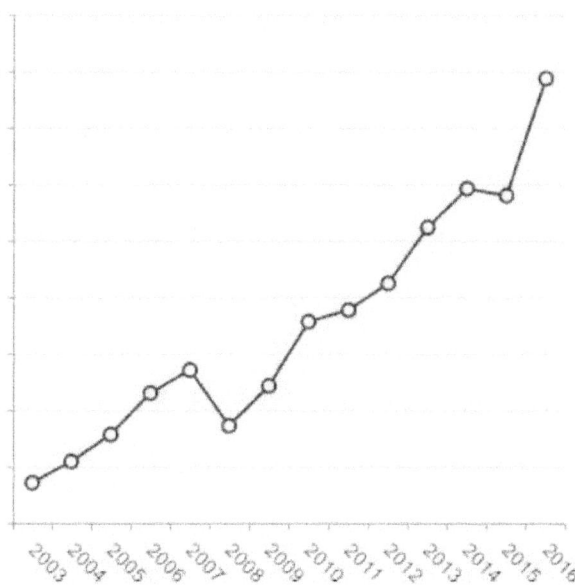

The increase in market value over time. Obviously, I've been making contributions to the account all along – in other words, this is not a chart of simple compounded returns. This graph doesn't go right back to the beginning, in 2001, either.

Returns per year. Note the high variations in return from year to year, which is normal. The big ugly crash was 2008. 2015 was also a losing year, but I didn't really notice because I wasn't really paying attention.

If you **do** pay too much attention, you'll be tempted to 'fiddle', and thereby lower your investment returns. This has been statistically proven. Google Terrance Odean and you'll see what I mean. And re-read this book!

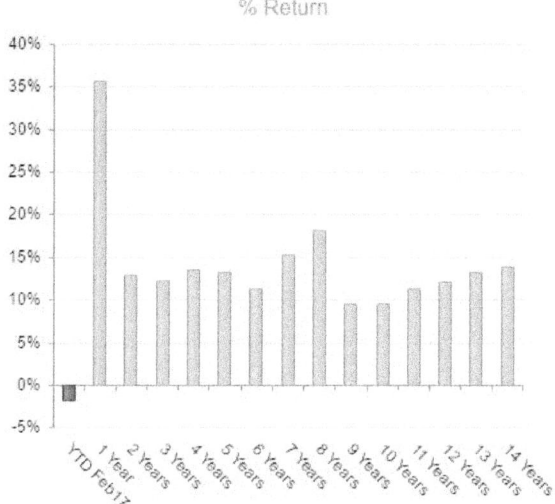

Returns, compounded. Last year was a 35% year. As you can see, the return averaged over time is just shy of 14%. YTD [year to date], I'm posting a negative return. Nothing to worry about, if past experience is anything to go by.

www.ingramcontent.com/pod-product-compliance
Lightning Source LLC
Chambersburg PA
CBHW061447180526
45170CB00004B/1593